FAMILY WORSHIP

FAMILY WORSHIP

A Selection of Bahá'í Prayers

✿

compiled by

Wendi Momen

GEORGE RONALD
OXFORD

GEORGE RONALD, Publisher
46 High Street, Kidlington, Oxford OX5 2DN

British Library Cataloguing in Publication Data

Family Worship: prayers revealed by Bahá'u'lláh,
the Báb and 'Abdu'l-Bahá.
1. Bahá'í life, Prayer
I. Momen, Wendi
297'.8943

ISBN 0–85398–289–9

Printed in Great Britain at the Alden Press, Oxford

CONTENTS

PRAYERS OF THE FAMILY

If love and agreement are manifest in a single family, that family will advance, become illumined and spiritual . . .

'Abdu'l-Bahá

Assistance

GLORY be to Thee, O my God! Thou hearest Thine ardent lovers lamenting in their separation from Thee, and such as have recognized Thee wailing because of their remoteness from Thy presence. Open Thou outwardly to their faces, O my Lord, the gates of Thy grace, that they may enter them by Thy leave and in conformity with Thy will, and may stand before the throne of Thy majesty, and catch the accents of Thy voice, and be illumined with the splendours of the light of Thy face.

Potent art Thou to do what pleaseth Thee. None can withstand the power of Thy sovereign might. From everlasting Thou wert alone, with none to equal Thee, and wilt unto everlasting remain far above all thought and every description of Thee. Have mercy, then, upon Thy servants by Thy grace and bounty, and suffer them not to be kept back from the shores of the ocean of Thy nearness. If Thou abandonest them, who is there to befriend them; and if Thou puttest them far from Thee, who is he that can favour them? They have none other Lord beside Thee, none to adore except Thyself. Deal Thou generously with them by Thy bountiful grace.

Thou, in truth, art the Ever-Forgiving, the Most Compassionate.

Bahá'u'lláh

GLORIFIED art Thou, O my God! I yield Thee thanks that Thou hast made known unto me Him who is the Dayspring of Thy mercy, and the Dawning-Place of Thy grace, and the Repository of Thy Cause. I beseech Thee by Thy Name, through which the faces of them that are nigh unto Thee have turned white, and the hearts of such as are devoted to Thee have winged their flight towards Thee, to grant that I may, at all times and under all conditions, lay

3

hold on Thy cord, and be rid of all attachment to anyone except Thee, and may keep mine eyes directed towards the horizon of Thy Revelation, and may carry out what Thou hast prescribed unto me in Thy Tablets.

Attire, O my Lord, both my inner and outer being with the raiment of Thy favours and Thy loving-kindness. Keep me safe, then, from whatsoever may be abhorrent unto Thee, and graciously assist me and my kindred to obey Thee, and to shun whatsoever may stir up any evil or corrupt desire within me.

Thou, truly, art the Lord of all mankind, and the Possessor of this world and of the next. No God is there save Thee, the All-Knowing, the All-Wise.

Bahá'u'lláh

GLORY be unto Thee, O Lord, Thou Who hast brought into being all created things, through the power of Thy behest.

O Lord! Assist those who have renounced all

else but Thee, and grant them a mighty victory. Send down upon them, O Lord, the concourse of the angels in heaven and earth and all that is between, to aid Thy servants, to succour and strengthen them, to enable them to achieve success, to sustain them, to invest them with glory, to confer upon them honour and exaltation, to enrich them and to make them triumphant with a wondrous triumph.

Thou art their Lord, the Lord of the heavens and the earth, the Lord of all the worlds. Strengthen this Faith, O Lord, through the power of these servants, and cause them to prevail over all the peoples of the world; for they, of a truth, are Thy servants who have detached themselves from aught else but Thee, and Thou, verily, art the protector of true believers.

Grant Thou, O Lord, that their hearts may, through allegiance to this, Thine inviolable Faith, grow stronger than anything else in the heavens and on earth and in whatsoever is between them; and strengthen, O Lord, their

hands with the tokens of Thy wondrous power
that they may manifest Thy power before the
gaze of all mankind.

The Báb

O THOU divine Providence, pitiful are we, grant
us Thy succour; homeless wanderers, give us
Thy shelter; scattered, do Thou unite us; astray,
gather us to Thy fold; bereft, do Thou bestow
upon us a share and portion; athirst, lead us to
the well-spring of Life; frail, strengthen us that
we may arise to help Thy Cause and offer
ourselves as a living sacrifice in the pathway of
guidance.

'Abdu'l-Bahá

LORD! Pitiful are we, grant us Thy favour; poor,
bestow upon us a share from the ocean of Thy
wealth; needy, do Thou satisfy us; abased, give
us Thy glory. The fowls of the air and the beasts
of the field receive their meat each day from

Thee, and all beings partake of Thy care and loving-kindness.

Deprive not this feeble one of Thy wondrous grace and vouchsafe by Thy might unto this helpless soul Thy bounty.

Give us our daily bread, and grant Thine increase in the necessities of life, that we may be dependent on none other but Thee, may commune wholly with Thee, may walk in Thy ways and declare Thy mysteries. Thou art the Almighty and the Loving and the Provider of all mankind.

'Abdu'l-Bahá

THOU seest me, O my God, bowed down in lowliness, humbling myself before Thy commandments, submitting to Thy sovereignty, trembling at the might of Thy dominion, fleeing from Thy wrath, entreating Thy grace, relying upon Thy forgiveness, shaking with awe at Thy fury. I implore Thee with a throbbing heart, with streaming tears and a yearning soul, and in complete detachment from all things, to make Thy lovers as rays of light across Thy realms, and to aid Thy chosen servants to exalt Thy Word, that their faces may turn beauteous and bright with splendour, that their hearts may be filled with mysteries, and that every soul may lay down its burden of sin. Guard them then from the aggressor, from him who hath become a shameless and blasphemous doer of wrong.

Verily, Thy lovers thirst, O my Lord; lead them to the wellspring of bounty and grace. Verily, they hunger; send down unto them Thy heavenly table. Verily, they are naked; robe them in the garments of learning and knowledge.

Heroes are they, O my Lord, lead them to the field of battle. Guides are they, make them to speak out with arguments and proofs. Ministering servants are they, cause them to pass round the cup that brimmeth with the wine of certitude. O my God, make them lions that crouch in the thickets, whales that plunge in the vasty deep.

Verily, Thou art He of abounding grace.
There is none other God save Thee, the Mighty,
the Powerful, the Ever-Bestowing.

'Abdu'l-Bahá

O GOD, my God! Aid Thou Thy trusted servants
to have loving and tender hearts. Help them to
spread, amongst all the nations of the earth, the
light of guidance that cometh from the Company on high. Verily Thou art the Strong, the
Powerful, the Mighty, the All-Subduing, the
Ever-Giving. Verily Thou art the Generous, the
Gentle, the Tender, the Most Bountiful.

'Abdu'l-Bahá

Firmness in the Covenant

I BESEECH Thee, O Thou Who art the Lord of
the worlds, and the Beloved of such as have
recognized Thee, and the Desire of all that are
in heaven and on earth, by Thy Name through
which the cry of every suppliant hath ascended
into the heaven of Thy transcendent holiness,
through which every seeker hath soared to the
sublimities of Thy unity and grandeur, through
which the imperfect have been perfected, and
the abased exalted, and the tongue of every
stammerer unloosed, and the sick made whole,
and whatever was unworthy of Thy highness and
beseemed not Thy greatness and Thy sovereignty made acceptable unto Thee — I beseech
Thee to aid us by Thine invisible hosts and
by a company of the angels of Thy Cause.
Do Thou, then, accept the works we have

performed for love of Thee, and for the sake of Thy pleasure. Cast us not away, O my God, from the door of Thy mercy, and break not our hopes in the wonders of Thy grace and favours.

Our limbs, our members, O my Lord, bear witness to Thy unity and oneness. Send down upon us Thy strength and power, that we may become steadfast in Thy Faith and may aid Thee among Thy servants. Illumine our eyes, O my Lord, with the effulgence of Thy beauty, and enlighten our hearts with the splendours of Thy knowledge and wisdom. Write us up, then, with those who have fulfilled their pledge to Thy Covenant in Thy days, and who, through their love for Thee, have detached themselves from the world and all that is therein.

Powerful art Thou to do what Thou pleasest. No God is there beside Thee, the All-Powerful, the Omniscient, the Supreme Ruler, the Help in Peril, the Self-Subsisting.

Bahá'u'lláh

SUFFER ME, O my God, to draw nigh unto Thee, and to abide within the precincts of Thy court, for remoteness from Thee hath well-nigh consumed me. Cause me to rest under the shadow of the wings of Thy grace, for the flame of my separation from Thee hath melted my heart within me. Draw me nearer unto the river that is life indeed, for my soul burneth with thirst in its ceaseless search after Thee. My sighs, O my God, proclaim the bitterness of mine anguish, and the tears I shed attest my love for Thee.

I beseech Thee, by the praise wherewith Thou praisest Thyself and the glory wherewith Thou glorifiest Thine own Essence, to grant that we may be numbered among them that have recognized Thee and acknowledged Thy sovereignty in Thy days. Help us then to quaff, O my God, from the fingers of mercy the living waters of Thy loving-kindness, that we may utterly forget all else except Thee, and be occupied only with Thy Self. Powerful art Thou to do what Thou willest. No God is there beside Thee, the

Mighty, the Help in Peril, the Self-Subsisting.

Glorified be Thy name, O Thou Who art the King of all Kings!

Bahá'u'lláh

I PRAY Thee, O Thou Who causest the dawn to appear, by Thy Name through Which Thou hast subjected the winds, and sent down Thy Tablets, that Thou wilt grant that we may draw near unto what Thou didst destine for us by Thy favour and bounty, and to be far removed from whatsoever may be repugnant unto Thee. Give us, then, to drink from the hands of Thy grace every day and every moment of our lives of the waters that are life indeed, O Thou Who art the Most Merciful! Make us, then, to be of them who helped Thee when fallen into the hands of those Thine enemies who are numbered with the rebellious among Thy creatures and the wicked amidst Thy people. Write down, then, for us the recompense ordained for him that hath attained Thy presence, and gazed on Thy

13

beauty, and supply us with every good thing ordained in Thy book for such of Thy creatures as enjoy near access to Thee.

Brighten our hearts, O my Lord, with the splendour of Thy knowledge, and illumine our sight with the light of such eyes as are fixed upon the horizon of Thy grace and the Day-spring of Thy glory. Preserve us, then, by Thy Most Great Name, Which Thou didst cause to overshadow such nations as lay claim to what Thou hast forbidden in Thy Book. This, verily, is what Thou didst announce unto us in Thy Scriptures and Thy Tablets.

Cause us, then, to be so steadfast in our love towards Thee that we will turn to none except Thee, and will be reckoned amongst them that are brought nigh to Thee, and acknowledge Thee as One Who is exalted above every comparison and is holy beyond all likeness, and will lift up our voices amongst Thy servants and cry aloud that He is the one God, the Incomparable, the Ever-Abiding, the Most Powerful, the All-Glorious, the All-Wise.

Bahá'u'lláh

O MY LORD and my Hope! Help Thou Thy loved ones to be steadfast in Thy mighty Covenant, to remain faithful to Thy manifest Cause, and to carry out the commandments Thou didst set down for them in Thy Book of Splendours; that they may become banners of guidance and lamps of the Company above, wellsprings of Thine infinite wisdom, and stars that lead aright, as they shine down from the supernal sky.

Verily, art Thou the Invincible, the Almighty, the All-Powerful.

'Abdu'l-Bahá

O LORD, my God! Assist Thy loved ones to be firm in Thy Faith, to walk in Thy ways, to be steadfast in Thy Cause. Give them Thy grace to withstand the onslaught of self and passion, to follow the light of Divine Guidance. Thou art the Powerful, the Gracious, the Self-Subsisting, the Bestower, the Compassionate, the Almighty, the All-Bountiful.

'Abdu'l-Bahá

MAKE firm our steps, O Lord! in Thy path and strengthen Thou our hearts in Thy obedience. Turn our faces toward the Beauty of Thy Oneness and gladden our bosoms with the signs of Thy Divine Unity. Adorn our bodies with the robe of Thy bounty and remove from our eyes the veil of sinfulness and give us the chalice of Thy grace, that the essence of all beings may sing Thy praise before the vision of Thy grandeur. Reveal then Thyself, O Lord! by Thy merciful utterance and the mystery of Thy Divine Being, that the holy ecstasy of prayer may fill our souls — a prayer that shall rise above words and letters and transcend the murmur of syllables and sounds — that all things may be merged into nothingness before the revelation of Thy splendour.

Lord! These are servants that have remained fast and firm in Thy Covenant and Thy Testament, that have held fast unto the cord of constancy in Thy Cause and clung unto the hem of the Robe of Thy grandeur. Assist them, O Lord! with Thy grace, confirm with Thy power

and strengthen their loins in obedience to Thee.
Thou art the Pardoner, the Gracious.

'Abdu'l-Bahá

HE IS GOD!

O Lord, my God, my Well-Beloved! These
are servants of Thine that have heard Thy Voice,
given ear to Thy Word and hearkened to Thy
Call. They have believed in Thee, witnessed
Thy wonders, acknowledged Thy proof and
testified to Thine evidence. They have walked
in Thy ways, followed Thy guidance, discovered
Thy mysteries, comprehended the secrets of Thy
Book, the verses of Thy Scrolls and the tidings
of Thy Epistles and Tablets. They have clung to
the hem of Thy garment and held fast unto the
robe of Thy light and grandeur. Their footsteps
have been strengthened in Thy Covenant and
their hearts made firm in Thy Testament. Lord!
Do Thou kindle in their hearts the flame of Thy
divine attraction and grant that the bird of love
and understanding may sing within their hearts.

Grant that they may be even as potent signs, re-splendent standards, and perfect as Thy Word. Exalt by them Thy Cause, unfurl Thy banners and publish far and wide Thy wonders. Make by them Thy Word triumphant and strengthen the loins of Thy loved ones. Unloose their tongues to laud Thy Name and inspire them to do Thy holy will and pleasure. Illumine their faces in Thy Kingdom of holiness and perfect their joy by aiding them to arise for the triumph of Thy Cause.

Lord! Feeble are we, strengthen us to diffuse the fragrances of Thy Holiness; poor, enrich us from the treasures of Thy Divine Unity; naked, clothe us with the robe of Thy bounty; sinful, forgive us our sins by Thy grace, Thy favour and Thy pardon. Thou art verily the Aider, the Helper, the Gracious, the Mighty, the Powerful.

The glory of glories rest upon them that are fast and firm.

'Abdu'l-Bahá

Forgiveness

PRAISE be unto Thee, O Lord! Forgive us our sins, have mercy upon us and enable us to return unto Thee. Suffer us not to rely on aught else besides Thee, and vouchsafe unto us, through Thy bounty, that which Thou lovest and desirest and well beseemeth Thee. Exalt the station of them that have truly believed, and forgive them with Thy gracious forgiveness. Verily, Thou art the Help in Peril, the Self-Subsisting.

The Báb

O GOD our Lord! Protect us through Thy grace from whatsoever may be repugnant unto Thee, and vouchsafe unto us that which well beseemeth Thee. Give us more out of Thy bounty, and bless us. Pardon us for the things we have done, and wash away our sins, and forgive us with Thy gracious forgiveness. Verily, Thou art the Most Exalted, the Self-Subsisting.

Thy loving providence hath encompassed all created things in the heavens and on the earth, and Thy forgiveness hath surpassed the whole creation. Thine is sovereignty; in Thy hand are the Kingdoms of Creation and Revelation; in Thy right hand Thou holdest all created things, and within Thy grasp are the assigned measures of forgiveness. Thou forgivest whomsoever among Thy servants Thou pleasest. Verily, Thou art the Ever-Forgiving, the All-Loving. Nothing whatsoever escapeth Thy knowledge, and naught is there which is hidden from Thee.

O God our Lord! Protect us through the potency of Thy might, enable us to enter Thy wondrous surging ocean, and grant us that which well befitteth Thee.

Thou art the Sovereign Ruler, the Mighty Doer, the Exalted, the All-Loving.

The Báb

O Thou forgiving Lord! Thou art the shelter of all these Thy servants. Thou knowest the secrets and art aware of all things. We are all helpless, and Thou art the Mighty, the Omnipotent. We are all sinners, and Thou art the Forgiver of sins, the Merciful, the Compassionate. O Lord! Look not at our shortcomings. Deal with us according to Thy grace and bounty. Our shortcomings are many, but the ocean of Thy forgiveness is boundless. Our weakness is grievous, but the evidences of Thine aid and assistance are clear. Therefore, confirm and strengthen us. Enable us to do that which is worthy of Thy holy Threshold. Illumine our hearts, grant us discerning eyes and attentive ears. Resuscitate the dead and heal the sick. Bestow wealth upon the poor and give peace and security to the fearful. Accept us in Thy kingdom and illumine us with the light of guidance. Thou art the Powerful and the Omnipotent. Thou art the Generous. Thou art the Clement. Thou art the Kind.

'Abdu'l-Bahá

Happiness

I GIVE thanks to Thee, O my God, that Thou hast suffered me to remember Thee. What else but remembrance of Thee can give delight to my soul or gladness to my heart? Communion with Thee enableth me to dispense with the remembrance of all Thy creatures, and my love for Thee empowereth me to endure the harm which my oppressors inflict upon me.

Send, therefore, unto my loved ones, O my God, what will cheer their hearts, and illumine their faces, and delight their souls. Thou knowest, O my Lord, that their joy is to behold the exaltation of Thy Cause and the glorification of Thy word. Do Thou unveil, therefore, O my God, what will gladden their eyes and ordain for them the good of this world and of the world which is to come.

Thou art, verily, the God of power, of strength and of bounty.

Bahá'u'lláh

O LORD! Render victorious Thy forbearing servants in Thy days by granting them a befitting victory, inasmuch as they have sought martyrdom in Thy path. Send down upon them that which will bring comfort to their minds, will rejoice their inner beings, will impart assurance to their hearts and tranquillity to their bodies and will enable their souls to ascend to the presence of God, the Most Exalted, and to attain the supreme Paradise and such retreats of glory as Thou hast destined for men of true knowledge and virtue. Verily, Thou knowest all things, while we are but Thy servants, Thy thralls, Thy bondsmen and Thy poor ones. No Lord but Thee do we invoke, O God our Lord, nor do we implore blessings or grace from anyone but Thee, O Thou Who art the God of mercy unto this world and the next. We are but the embodiments of poverty, of nothingness, of helplessness and of perdition, while Thy whole Being betokeneth wealth, independence, glory, majesty and boundless grace.

Turn our recompense, O Lord, into that which well beseemeth Thee of the good of this world and of the next, and of the manifold bounties which extend from on high down to the earth below.

Verily, Thou art our Lord and the Lord of all things. Into Thy hands do we surrender ourselves, yearning for the things that pertain unto Thee.

The Báb

PRAISED and glorified art Thou, O God! Grant that the day of attaining Thy holy presence may be fast approaching. Cheer our hearts through the potency of Thy love and good-pleasure and bestow upon us steadfastness that we may willingly submit to Thy Will and Thy Decree. Verily Thy knowledge embraceth all the things Thou hast created or wilt create and Thy celestial might transcendeth whatsoever Thou hast alled or wilt call into being. There is none to

worshipped but Thee, there is none to be

ed except Thee, there is none to be adored

es Thee and there is naught to be loved

hy good-pleasure.

ly Thou art the supreme Ruler, the

n Truth, the Help in Peril, the Self-

ave   g.

nd

th.

kies

and

they

hee,

r the

                                          The Báb

Ever-

-*Bahá*

In Praise of God

O THOU loving Provider! These souls h[ave]
hearkened to the summons of the Kingdom, [and]
have gazed upon the glory of the Sun of Tru[th].
They have risen upward to the refreshing s[ky]
of love; they are enamoured of Thy nature, [and]
they worship Thy beauty. Unto Thee have [they]
turned themselves, speaking together of T[hee],
seeking out Thy dwelling, and thirsting fo[r the]
waterbrooks of Thy heavenly realm.

Thou art the Giver, the Bestower, the [ever-]
loving.

'Abdu'l[-Bahá]

Protection

ALL PRAISE be to Thee, O my God, for the things Thou didst ordain for me through Thy decree and by the power of Thy sovereignty. I beseech Thee that Thou wilt fortify both myself and them that love me in our love for Thee, and wilt keep us firm in Thy Cause. I swear by Thy might! O my God! Thy servant's shame is to be shut out as by a veil from Thee, and his glory is to know Thee. Armed with the power of Thy name nothing can ever hurt me, and with Thy love in my heart all the world's afflictions can in no wise alarm me.

Send down, therefore, O my Lord, upon me and upon my loved ones that which will protect us from the mischief of those that have repudiated Thy truth and disbelieved in Thy signs.

Thou art, verily, the All-Glorious, the Most Bountiful.

Bahá'u'lláh

GLORY be to Thee, O my God! I beg of Thee by Thy name, the Most Merciful, to protect Thy servants and Thy handmaidens when the tempests of trials pass over them, and Thy manifold tests assail them. Enable them, then, O my God, so to seek refuge within the stronghold of Thy love and of Thy Revelation, that neither Thine adversaries nor the wicked doers among Thy servants, who have broken Thy Covenant and Thy Testament, and turned away most disdainfully from the Day-Spring of Thine Essence and the Revealer of Thy glory, may prevail against them.

They themselves, O my Lord, have waited at the door of Thy grace. Do Thou open it to their faces with the keys of Thy bountiful favours. Potent art Thou to do what Thou willest, and to ordain what Thou pleasest. These are the ones, O my Lord, who have set their faces towards Thee, and turned unto Thy habitation. Do with them, therefore, as becometh Thy mercy, which hath surpassed the worlds.

Bahá'u'lláh

LAUDED be Thy name, O my God! Thou beholdest how the tempestuous winds of tests have caused the steadfast in faith to tremble, and how the breath of trials hath stirred up those whose hearts had been firmly established, except such as have partaken of the Wine that is life indeed from the hands of the Manifestation of Thy name, the Most Merciful. These are the ones whom no word except Thy most exalted word can move, whom nothing whatever save the sweet smelling fragrance of the robe of Thy remembrance can enrapture, O Thou Who art the Possessor of all names and the Maker of earth and heaven!

I implore Thee, O Thou Who art the beloved Companion of Bahá, by Thy name, the All-Glorious, to keep safe these Thy servants under the shadow of the wings of Thine all-encompassing mercy, that the darts of the evil suggestions of the wicked doers among Thy creatures, who have disbelieved in Thy signs, may be kept back from them. No one on earth, O my Lord, can withstand Thy power, and none in all the kingdom of Thy names is able to frustrate Thy purpose. Show forth, then, the power of Thy sovereignty and of Thy dominion, and teach Thy loved ones what beseemeth them in Thy days.

Thou art, verily, the Almighty, the Most Exalted, the All-Glorious, the Most Great.

Bahá'u'lláh

O MY God and my Master! I am Thy servant and the son of Thy servant. I have risen from my couch at this dawn-tide when the Day-Star of Thy oneness hath shone forth from the Day-spring of Thy will, and hath shed its radiance upon the whole world, according to what had been ordained in the Books of Thy Decree.

Praise be unto Thee, O my God, that we have wakened to the splendours of the light of Thy knowledge. Send down, then, upon us, O my Lord, what will enable us to dispense with any one but Thee, and will rid us of all attachment to aught except Thyself. Write down, moreover, for me, and for such as are dear to me, and for my kindred, man and woman alike, the good of this world and the world to come. Keep us safe, then, through Thine unfailing protection, O Thou the Beloved of the entire creation and the Desire of the whole universe, from them whom Thou hast made to be the manifestations of the Evil Whisperer, who whisper in men's breasts. Potent art Thou to do Thy pleasure. Thou art, verily, the Almighty, the Help in Peril, the Self-Subsisting.

Bless Thou, O Lord my God, Him Whom Thou hast set over Thy most excellent Titles, and through Whom Thou hast divided between the godly and the wicked, and graciously aid us to do what Thou lovest and desirest. Bless Thou, moreover, O my God, them Who are Thy Words and Thy Letters, and them who have set their faces towards Thee, and turned unto Thy face, and hearkened to Thy Call.

Thou art, truly, the Lord and King of all men and art potent over all things.

Bahá'u'lláh

LAUDED be Thy name, O Lord my God! I entreat Thee by Thy Name through which the Hour hath struck, and the Resurrection came to pass, and fear and trembling seized all that are in heaven and all that are on earth, to rain down, out of the heaven of Thy mercy and the clouds of Thy tender compassion, what will gladden the hearts of Thy servants, who have turned towards Thee and helped Thy Cause.

Keep safe Thy servants and Thy handmaidens, O my Lord, from the darts of idle fancy and vain imaginings, and give them from the hands of Thy grace a draught of the soft-flowing waters of Thy knowledge.

Thou, truly, art the Almighty, the Most Exalted, the Ever-Forgiving, the Most Generous.

Bahá'u'lláh

O GOD, my God! Shield Thy trusted servants from the evils of self and passion, protect them with the watchful eye of Thy loving-kindness from all rancour, hate and envy, shelter them in the impregnable stronghold of Thy care and, safe from the darts of doubtfulness, make them the manifestations of Thy glorious signs, illumine their faces with the effulgent rays shed from the Dayspring of Thy divine unity, gladden their hearts with the verses revealed from Thy holy kingdom, strengthen their loins by Thine all-swaying power that cometh from Thy realm of glory. Thou art the All-Bountiful, the Protector, the Almighty, the Gracious.

'Abdu'l-Bahá

Spiritual Progress

O THOU forgiving God! These servants are turning to Thy kingdom and seeking Thy grace and bounty. O God! Make their hearts good and pure in order that they may become worthy of Thy love. Purify and sanctify the spirits that the light of the Sun of Reality may shine through them. Purify and sanctify the eyes that they may perceive Thy lights. Purify and sanctify the ears in order that they may hear the call of Thy kingdom. O Lord! Verily, we are weak, but Thou art mighty. Verily, we are poor, but Thou art rich. We are seekers, and Thou art the One sought. O Lord! Have compassion upon us and forgive us; bestow upon us capacity and readiness in order that we may be responsive to Thy favours, attracted to Thy kingdom, enkindled with the fire of Thy love, and resuscitated through the breaths of Thy Holy Spirit in this radiant century. Thou art Powerful! Thou art Almighty! Thou art Merciful! and Thou art Most Generous!

'Abdu'l-Bahá

O THOU kind Lord! Praise be unto Thee that Thou hast shown us the highway of guidance, opened the doors of the kingdom and manifested Thyself through the Sun of Reality. To the blind Thou hast given sight; to the deaf Thou hast granted hearing; Thou hast resuscitated the dead; Thou hast enriched the poor; Thou hast shown the way to those who have gone astray; Thou hast led those with parched lips to the fountain of guidance; Thou hast suffered the thirsty fish to reach the ocean of reality and Thou hast invited the wandering birds to the rose-garden of grace.

O Thou Almighty! We are Thy servants and Thy poor ones; we are remote and yearn for Thy presence; are athirst for the water of Thy fountain; are ill, longing for Thy healing. We are walking in Thy path and have no aim or hope save the diffusion of Thy fragrance, so that all souls raise the cry of, 'O God, guide us to the straight path.' May their eyes be opened to behold the light, and may they be freed from the darkness of ignorance. May they gather around the lamp of Thy guidance. May every portionless one receive a share. May the deprived ones become the confidants of Thy mysteries.

O Almighty! Look upon us with the glance of mercifulness. Grant us heavenly confirmation. Bestow upon us the breath of the Holy Spirit, so that we may be assisted in Thy service and, like unto brilliant stars, shine in these regions with the light of Thy guidance.

Verily, Thou art the Powerful, the Mighty, the Wise and the Seeing.

'Abdu'l-Bahá

O MY GOD! O my God! Verily, these servants are turning to Thee, supplicating Thy kingdom of mercy. Verily, they are attracted by Thy holiness and set aglow with the fire of Thy love,

seeking confirmation from Thy wondrous kingdom and hoping for attainment in Thy heavenly
realm. Verily, they long for the descent of Thy
bestowal, desiring illumination from the Sun of
Reality. O Lord! Make them radiant lamps,
merciful signs, fruitful trees and shining stars.
May they come forth in Thy service and be
connected with Thee by the bonds and ties of
Thy love, longing for the lights of Thy favour.
O Lord! Make them signs of guidance, standards
of Thy immortal kingdom, waves of the sea of
Thy mercy, mirrors of the light of Thy majesty.
Verily, Thou art the Generous! Verily, Thou art
the Merciful! Verily, Thou art the Precious, the
Beloved!

'Abdu'l-Bahá

O LORD! We are weak; strengthen us. O God!
We are ignorant; make us knowing. O Lord! We
are poor; make us wealthy. O God! We are dead;
quicken us. O Lord! We are humiliation itself;
glorify us in Thy kingdom. If Thou dost assist
us, O Lord, we shall become as scintillating

stars. If Thou dost not assist us, we shall become lower than the earth. O Lord! Strengthen us. O God! Confer victory upon us. O God! Enable us to conquer self and overcome desire. O Lord! Deliver us from the bondage of the material world. O Lord! Quicken us through the breath of the Holy Spirit in order that we may arise to serve Thee, engage in worshipping Thee, and exert ourselves in Thy kingdom with the utmost sincerity. O Lord, Thou art Powerful! O God, Thou art Forgiving! O Lord, Thou art Compassionate! *'Abdu'l-Bahá*

GLORY be to Thee, O God, for Thy manifestation of love to mankind! O Thou Who art our Life and Light, guide Thy servants in Thy way, and make us rich in Thee and free from all save Thee.

O God, teach us Thy Oneness and give us a realization of Thy Unity, that we may see no one save Thee. Thou art the Merciful and the Giver of bounty!

O God, create in the hearts of Thy beloved

the fire of Thy love, that it may consume the thought of everything save Thee.

Reveal to us, O God, Thine exalted eternity — that Thou hast ever been and wilt ever be, and that there is no God save Thee. Verily, in Thee will we find comfort and strength.

'Abdu'l-Bahá

O THOU Whose tests are a healing medicine to such as are nigh unto Thee, Whose sword is the ardent desire of all them that love Thee, Whose dart is the dearest wish of those hearts that yearn after Thee, Whose decree is the sole hope of them that have recognized Thy truth! I implore Thee, by Thy divine sweetness and by the splendours of the glory of Thy face, to send down upon us from Thy retreats on high that which will enable us to draw nigh unto Thee. Set, then, our feet firm, O my God, in Thy Cause, and enlighten our hearts with the effulgence of Thy knowledge, and illumine our breasts with the brightness of Thy names.

'Abdu'l-Bahá

HE IS GOD!

O God, my God! These are servants attracted in Thy days by the fragrances of Thy holiness, enkindled with the flame burning in Thy holy tree, responding to Thy voice, uttering Thy praise, awakened by Thy breeze, stirred by Thy sweet savours, beholding Thy signs, understanding Thy verses, hearkening to Thy words, believing Thy Revelation and assured of Thy lovingkindness. Their eyes, O Lord, are fixed upon Thy kingdom of effulgent glory and their faces turned toward Thy dominion on high, their hearts beating with the love of Thy radiant and glorious beauty, their souls consumed with the flame of Thy love, O Lord of this world and the world hereafter, their lives seething with the ardour of their longing for Thee, and their tears poured forth for Thy sake.

Shield them within the stronghold of Thy protection and safety, preserve them in Thy watchful care, look upon them with the eyes of Thy providence and mercy, make them the signs of Thy divine unity that are manifest throughout all regions, the standards of Thy might that wave above Thy mansions of grandeur, the shining lamps that burn with the oil of Thy wisdom in the globes of Thy guidance, the birds of the garden of Thy knowledge that warble upon the topmost boughs in Thy sheltering paradise, and the leviathans of the ocean of Thy bounty that plunge by Thy supreme mercy in the fathomless deeps.

O Lord, my God! Lowly are these servants of Thine, exalt them in Thy kingdom on high; feeble, strengthen them by Thy supreme power; abased, bestow upon them Thy glory in Thine all-highest realm; poor, enrich them in Thy great dominion. Do Thou then ordain for them all the good Thou hast destined in Thy worlds, visible and invisible, prosper them in this world below, gladden their hearts with Thine inspiration, O Lord of all beings! Illumine their hearts with Thy joyful tidings diffused from Thine all-glorious Station, make firm their steps in Thy Most Great Covenant and strengthen their loins in Thy firm Testament, by Thy bounty and promised grace, O Gracious and Merciful One! Thou art, verily, the Gracious, the All-Bountiful.

'Abdu'l-Bahá

O THOU kind Lord! We are servants of Thy Threshold, taking shelter at Thy holy Door. We seek no refuge save only this strong pillar, turn nowhere for a haven but unto Thy safekeeping. Protect us, bless us, support us, make us such that we shall love but Thy good pleasure, utter only Thy praise, follow only the pathway of truth, that we may become rich enough to dispense with all save Thee, and receive our gifts from the sea of Thy beneficence, that we may ever strive to exalt Thy Cause and to spread Thy sweet savours far and wide, that we may become oblivious of self and occupied only with Thee, and disown all else and be caught up in Thee.

O Thou Provider, O Thou Forgiver! Grant us Thy grace and loving-kindness, Thy gifts and Thy bestowals, and sustain us, that we may attain our goal. Thou art the Powerful,

the Able, the Knower, the Seer; and verily
Thou art the Generous, and verily Thou art the
All-Merciful, and verily Thou art the Ever-
Forgiving, He to Whom repentance is due, He
Who forgiveth even the most grievous of sins.

'Abdu'l-Bahá

O MY GOD! O my God! Verily, Thou dost
perceive those who are present here turning unto
Thee, relying upon Thee. O my Lord! O my
Lord! Illumine their eyes by the light of love,
and enkindle their hearts by the rays streaming
from the heaven of the Supreme Concourse.
Suffer them to become the signs of Thy bestowal
amongst the people and the standards of Thy
grace amongst mankind. O Lord! Make those
who are here the hosts of heaven, and through
their service and instrumentality subdue the
hearts of humanity. Cause Thy great mercy to
descend upon them, and render all Thy friends
victorious. Direct them that they may turn
toward Thy kingdom of mercy and proclaim
Thy name among the people. May they lead

the people to the bounty of Thy most great guidance.

O Lord! O Lord! Cast the glance of Thy mercy upon them all.

O Lord! O Lord! Ordain for them the beauty of Thy holiness in Thy Kingdom of eternity.

O Lord! O Lord! Protect them in every test, make every foot firm in the pathway of Thy love, and help them to be as mighty mountains in Thy Cause so that their faith shall not be wavering, their sight shall not be dimmed nor hindered from witnessing the lights emanating from Thy supreme Kingdom. Verily, Thou art the Generous. Thou art the Almighty. Verily, Thou art the Clement, the Merciful.

'Abdu'l-Bahá

O GOD, my God! These are Thy feeble servants; they are Thy loyal bondsmen and Thy handmaidens, who have bowed themselves down before Thine exalted Utterance and humbled themselves at Thy Threshold of light, and borne witness to Thy oneness through which the Sun hath been made to shine in midday splendour. They have listened to the summons Thou didst raise from out Thy hidden Realm, and with hearts quivering with love and rapture, they have responded to Thy call.

O Lord, shower upon them all the outpourings of Thy mercy, rain down upon them all the waters of Thy grace. Make them to grow as beauteous plants in the garden of heaven, and from the full and brimming clouds of Thy bestowals and out of the deep pools of Thine abounding grace make Thou this garden to flower, and keep it ever green and lustrous, ever fresh and shimmering and fair.

Thou art, verily, the Mighty, the Exalted, the Powerful, He Who alone, in the heavens and on the earth, abideth unchanged. There is none other God save Thee, the Lord of manifest tokens and signs.

'Abdu'l-Bahá

Unity

O MY GOD! O my God! Unite the hearts of Thy
servants, and reveal to them Thy great purpose.
May they follow Thy commandments and abide
in Thy law. Help them, O God, in their
endeavour, and grant them strength to serve
Thee. O God! Leave them not to themselves,
but guide their steps by the light of Thy
knowledge, and cheer their hearts by Thy love.
Verily, Thou art their Helper and their Lord.

Bahá'u'lláh

O MY GOD! O my God! Verily, these are
servants at the threshold of Thy mercy, and
maidservants at the door of Thy oneness. Verily,
they have gathered in this temple to turn to Thy
face of glory, holding to the hem of Thy
garment and to Thy singleness, seeking Thy

good pleasure and ascent into Thy Kingdom. They receive effulgence from the Sun of Reality in this glorious century, and they long for Thy goodwill in all great affairs. O Lord! Illumine their sight with a vision of Thy signs and riches, and quicken their ears with hearkening to Thy Word. Render their hearts replete with Thy love, and gladden their spirits with Thy meeting. Deign to bestow upon them spiritual good in Thine earth and heaven, and make them signs of unity among Thy servants in order that the real unity may appear and all may become one in Thy Cause and Kingdom. Verily, Thou art the Generous. Verily, Thou art the Mighty, the Spiritual. Thou art the Merciful, the Clement.   *'Abdu'l-Bahá*

O MY GOD! O my God! Verily, I invoke Thee and supplicate before Thy threshold, asking Thee that all Thy mercies may descend upon these souls. Specialize them for Thy favour and Thy truth.

  O Lord! Unite and bind together the hearts,

join in accord all the souls, and exhilarate the spirits through the signs of Thy sanctity and oneness. O Lord! Make these faces radiant through the light of Thy oneness. Strengthen the loins of Thy servants in the service of Thy kingdom.

O Lord, Thou possessor of infinite mercy! O Lord of forgiveness and pardon! Forgive our sins, pardon our shortcomings, and cause us to turn to the kingdom of Thy clemency, invoking the kingdom of might and power, humble at Thy shrine and submissive before the glory of Thine evidences.

O Lord God! Make us as waves of the sea, as flowers of the garden, united, agreed through the bounties of Thy love. O Lord! Dilate the breasts through the signs of Thy oneness, and make all mankind as stars shining from the same height of glory, as perfect fruits growing upon Thy tree of life.

Verily, Thou art the Almighty, the Self-Subsistent, the Giver, the Forgiving, the Pardoner, the Omniscient, the One Creator.

'Abdu'l-Bahá

PRAYERS FOR THE HOME

Blessed is the house that hath attained unto My tender mercy, wherein My remembrance is celebrated . . .

Bahá'u'lláh

BLESSED is the spot, and the house, and the place, and the city, and the heart, and the mountain, and the refuge, and the cave, and the valley, and the land, and the sea, and the island, and the meadow where mention of God hath been made, and His praise glorified.

Bahá'u'lláh

BLESSED is the house that hath attained unto My tender mercy, wherein My remembrance is celebrated, and which is ennobled by the presence of My loved ones, who have proclaimed My praise, cleaved fast to the cord of My grace and been honoured by chanting My verses. Verily they are the exalted servants whom God hath extolled in the Qayyumu'l-Asmá and other scriptures. Verily He is the All-Hearing, the Answerer, He Who perceiveth all things.

Bahá'u'lláh

O MY GOD! Let the outpourings of Thy bounty and blessings descend upon homes whose inmates have embraced Thy Faith, as a token of Thy grace and as a mark of loving-kindness from Thy presence. Verily unsurpassed art Thou in granting forgiveness. Should Thy bounty be withheld from anyone, how could he be reckoned among the followers of the Faith in Thy Day?

Bless me, O my God, and those who will believe in Thy signs on the appointed Day, and such as cherish my love in their hearts — a love which Thou dost instil into them. Verily Thou art the Lord of righteousness, the Most Exalted.

The Báb

I BESEECH GOD to graciously make of thy home a centre for the diffusion of the light of divine guidance, for the dissemination of the Words of God and for enkindling at all times the fire of love in the hearts of His faithful servants and maidservants. Know thou of a certainty that every house wherein the anthem of praise is

raised to the Realm of Glory in celebration of
the Name of God is indeed a heavenly home,
and one of the gardens of delight in the Paradise
of God.

'Abdu'l-Bahá

MY home is the home of peace.
My home is the home of joy and delight.
My home is the home of laughter and exultation.
Whosoever enters through the portals of this
    home,
  must go out with gladsome heart.
This is the home of light;
  whosoever enters here must become illumined.
This is the home of knowledge:
  the one who enters it must receive knowledge.
This is the home of love:
  those who come in must learn the lessons of
    love;
  thus may they know how to love each other.

'Abdu'l-Bahá

PRAYERS OF PARENTS
FOR THEIR CHILDREN

Children must be most carefully watched over, protected and trained; in such consisteth true parenthood and parental mercy.

'Abdu'l-Bahá

Education

O GOD! Educate these children. These children are the plants of Thine orchard, the flowers of Thy meadow, the roses of Thy garden. Let Thy rain fall upon them; let the Sun of Reality shine upon them with Thy love. Let Thy breeze refresh them in order that they may be trained, grow and develop, and appear in the utmost beauty. Thou art the Giver. Thou art the Compassionate.

'Abdu'l-Bahá

O THOU kind Lord! These lovely children are the handiwork of the fingers of Thy might and wondrous signs of Thy greatness. O God! Protect these children, graciously assist them to be educated and enable them to render service to the world of humanity. O God! These children are pearls, cause them to be nurtured within the shell of Thy loving-kindness.

Thou art the Bountiful, the All-Loving.

'Abdu'l-Bahá

Healing

THOU ART HE, O my God, through Whose names the sick are healed and the ailing are restored, and the thirsty are given drink, and the sore-vexed are tranquillized, and the wayward are guided, and the abased are exalted, and the poor are enriched, and the ignorant are enlightened, and the gloomy are illumined, and the sorrowful are cheered, and the chilled are warmed, and the downtrodden are raised up. Through Thy name, O my God, all created things were stirred up, and the heavens were spread, and the earth was established, and the clouds were raised and made to rain upon the earth. This, verily, is a token of Thy grace unto all Thy creatures.

I implore Thee, therefore, by Thy name through which Thou didst manifest Thy Godhead, and didst exalt Thy Cause above all creation, and by each of Thy most excellent titles and most august attributes, and by all the virtues wherewith Thy transcendent and most exalted Being is extolled, to send down this night from the clouds of Thy mercy the rains of Thy healing upon this suckling, whom Thou hast related unto Thine all-glorious Self in the kingdom of Thy creation. Clothe him, then, O my God, by Thy grace, with the robe of well-being and health, and guard him, O my Beloved, from every affliction and disorder, and from whatever is obnoxious unto Thee. Thy might, verily, is equal to all things. Thou, in truth, art the Most Powerful, the Self-Subsisting. Send down, moreover, upon him, O my God, the good of this world and of the next, and the good of the former and latter generations. Thy might and Thy wisdom are, verily, equal unto this.

Bahá'u'lláh

Infants

PRAISED be Thou, O Lord my God! Graciously grant that this infant be fed from the breast of Thy tender mercy and loving providence and be nourished with the fruit of Thy celestial trees. Suffer him not to be committed to the care of anyone save Thee, inasmuch as Thou, Thyself, through the potency of Thy sovereign will and power, didst create and call him into being. There is none other God but Thee, the Almighty, the All-Knowing.

Lauded art Thou, O my Best Beloved, waft over him the sweet savours of Thy transcendent bounty and the fragrances of Thy holy bestowals. Enable him then to seek shelter beneath the shadow of Thy most exalted Name, O Thou Who holdest in Thy grasp the kingdom of names and attributes. Verily, Thou art potent to do what Thou willest, and Thou art indeed the Mighty, the Exalted, the Ever-Forgiving, the Gracious, the Generous, the Merciful.

Bahá'u'lláh

O THOU peerless Lord! Let this suckling babe be nursed from the breast of Thy loving-kindness, guard it within the cradle of Thy safety and protection and grant that it may be reared in the arms of Thy tender affection.

'Abdu'l-Bahá

O GOD! Rear this little babe in the bosom of Thy love, and give it milk from the breast of Thy Providence. Cultivate this fresh plant in the rose garden of Thy love and aid it to grow through the showers of Thy bounty. Make it a child of the kingdom, and lead it to Thy heavenly realm. Thou art powerful and kind, and Thou art the Bestower, the Generous, the Lord of surpassing bounty.

'Abdu'l-Bahá

Spiritual Progress

HE IS GOD!

O Thou pure God! Let these saplings which have sprouted by the stream of Thy guidance become fresh and verdant through the outpourings of the clouds of Thy tender mercy; cause them to be stirred by the gentle winds wafting from the meads of Thy oneness and cause them to be revived through the rays of the Sun of Reality, that they may continually grow and flourish, and burst into blossoms and fruit.

O Lord God! Bestow upon each one understanding; give them power and strength and cause them to mirror forth Thy divine aid and confirmation, so that they may become highly distinguished among the people.

Thou art the Mighty and the Powerful.

'Abdu'l-Bahá

Prayers of Children

Teach unto your children the words that have been sent down from God, that they may recite them in the sweetest of tones.

Bahá'u'lláh

For Parents

O GOD, my God! I implore Thee by the blood
of Thy true lovers who were so enraptured by
Thy sweet utterance that they hastened unto the
Pinnacle of Glory, the site of the most glorious
martyrdom, and I beseech Thee by the mysteries
which lie enshrined in Thy knowledge and by
the pearls that are treasured in the ocean of
Thy bounty to grant forgiveness unto me and
unto my father and my mother. Of those who
show forth mercy, Thou art in truth the Most
Merciful. No God is there but Thee, the Ever-
Forgiving, the All-Bountiful.

Bahá'u'lláh

IT IS seemly that the servant should, after each
prayer, supplicate God to bestow mercy and

64

forgiveness upon his parents. Thereupon God's call will be raised: 'Thousand upon thousand of what thou hast asked for thy parents shall be thy recompense!' Blessed is he who remembereth his parents when communing with God. There is, verily, no God but Him, the Mighty, the Well-Beloved.

The Báb

I BEG forgiveness, O my God, and implore pardon after the manner Thou wishest Thy servants to direct themselves to Thee. I beg of Thee to wash away our sins as befitteth Thy Lordship, and to forgive me, my parents, and those who in Thy estimation have entered the abode of Thy love in a manner which is worthy of Thy transcendent sovereignty and well beseemeth the glory of Thy celestial power.

O my God! Thou hast inspired my soul to offer its supplication to Thee, and but for Thee, I would not call upon Thee. Lauded and glorified art Thou; I yield Thee praise inasmuch as Thou didst reveal Thyself unto me, and I beg

Thee to forgive me, since I have fallen short in my duty to know Thee and have failed to walk in the path of Thy love.

The Báb

O LORD! In this Most Great Dispensation Thou dost accept the intercession of children in behalf of their parents. This is one of the special infinite bestowals of this Dispensation. Therefore, O Thou kind Lord, accept the request of this Thy servant at the threshold of Thy singleness and submerge his father in the ocean of Thy grace, because this son hath arisen to render Thee service and is exerting effort at all times in the pathway of Thy love. Verily, Thou art the Giver, the Forgiver and the Kind!

'Abdu'l-Bahá

Spiritual Progress

GLORIFIED art Thou, O Lord my God! I give Thee thanks inasmuch as Thou hast called me into being in Thy days, and infused into me Thy love and Thy knowledge. I beseech Thee, by Thy name whereby the goodly pearls of Thy wisdom and Thine utterance were brought forth out of the treasuries of the hearts of such of Thy servants as are nigh unto Thee, and through which the Day-Star of Thy name, the Compassionate, hath shed its radiance upon all that are in Thy heaven and on Thy earth, to supply me, by Thy grace and bounty, with Thy wondrous and hidden bounties.

These are the earliest days of my life, O my God, which Thou hast linked with Thine own days. Now that Thou hast conferred upon me so great an honour, withhold not from me the things Thou hast ordained for Thy chosen ones.

I am, O my God, but a tiny seed which Thou hast sown in the soil of Thy love, and caused to spring forth by the hand of Thy bounty. This seed craveth, therefore, in its inmost being, for the waters of Thy mercy and the living fountain of Thy grace. Send down upon it, from the heaven of Thy loving-kindness, that which will enable it to flourish beneath Thy shadow and within the borders of Thy court. Thou art He Who watereth the hearts of all that have recognized Thee from Thy plenteous stream and the fountain of Thy living waters.

Praised be God, the Lord of the worlds.

Bahá'u'lláh

O GOD, guide me, protect me, make of me a shining lamp and a brilliant star. Thou art the Mighty and the Powerful.

'Abdu'l-Bahá

HE IS GOD!

O my God! O my God!

Thou seest these children who are the twigs of the tree of life, the birds of the meads of salvation, the pearls of the ocean of Thy grace, the roses of the garden of Thy guidance. O God, our Lord: We sing Thy praise, bear witness to Thy sanctity and implore fervently the heaven of Thy mercy to make us lights of guidance, stars shining above the horizons of eternal glory amongst mankind and to teach us a knowledge which proceedeth from Thee. Yá Bahá'u'l-Abhá!

'Abdu'l-Bahá

HE IS GOD!

O Thou compassionate Lord! O Lord of Hosts! Praise be unto Thee that Thou hast preferred these young children over the full grown and the matured, hast endowed them with Thy special bounty, hast guided them, hast bestowed upon them Thy light and hast given them spirituality. Confirm us so that when we attain maturity we may be enabled to serve Thy

Kingdom, may train the souls, may become
ignited candles and may shine like unto stars.
Thou art the Giver, the Bestower and the Kind.

'Abdu'l-Bahá

O PEERLESS LORD! Be Thou a shelter for this
poor child and a kind and forgiving Master unto
this erring and unhappy soul. O Lord! Though
we are but worthless plants, yet we belong to
Thy garden of roses. Though saplings without
leaves and blossoms, yet we are a part of Thine
orchard. Nurture this plant then through the
outpourings of the clouds of Thy tender mercy
and quicken and refresh this sapling through the
reviving breath of Thy spiritual springtime.
Suffer him to become heedful, discerning and
noble, and grant that he may attain eternal life
and abide in Thy Kingdom for evermore.

'Abdu'l-Bahá

O THOU Lord of wondrous grace! Bestow upon
us new blessing. Give to us the freshness of the

spring. We are saplings which have been planted by the fingers of Thy bounty and have been formed out of the water and clay of Thy tender affection. We thirst for the living waters of Thy favours and are dependent upon the outpourings of the clouds of Thy generosity. Abandon not to itself this grove wherein our hopes aspire, nor withhold therefrom the showers of Thy loving-kindness. Grant that from the clouds of Thy mercy may fall copious rain so that the trees of our lives may bring forth fruit and we may attain the most cherished desire of our hearts.

'Abdu'l-Bahá

O LORD! Make these children excellent plants. Let them grow and develop in the Garden of Thy Covenant, and bestow freshness and beauty through the outpourings of the clouds of the Abhá Kingdom.

O Thou kind Lord! I am a little child, exalt me by admitting me to the kingdom. I am earthly, make me heavenly; I am of the world below, let me belong to the realm above;

gloomy, suffer me to become radiant; material, make me spiritual, and grant that I may manifest Thine infinite bounties.

Thou art the Powerful, the All-Loving.

'Abdu'l-Bahá

O MY LORD! O my Lord!

I am a child of tender years. Nourish me from the breast of Thy love, educate me in the school of Thy guidance and develop me under the shadow of Thy bounty. Deliver me from darkness, make me a brilliant light; free me from unhappiness, make me a flower of the rose garden; suffer me to become a servant of Thy threshold and confer upon me the disposition and nature of the righteous; make me a cause of bounty to the human world, and crown my head with the diadem of eternal life.

Verily, Thou art the Powerful, the Mighty, the Seer, the Hearer.

'Abdu'l-Bahá

PRAYER FOR YOUTH

Wherefore, O ye illumined youth, strive by night and by day to unravel the mysteries of the mind and spirit, and to grasp the secrets of the Day of God.

'Abdu'l-Bahá

O LORD! Make this youth radiant, and confer Thy bounty upon this poor creature. Bestow upon him knowledge, grant him added strength at the break of every morn and guard him within the shelter of Thy protection so that he may be freed from error, may devote himself to the service of Thy Cause, may guide the wayward, lead the hapless, free the captives and awaken the heedless, that all may be blessed with Thy remembrance and praise. Thou art the Mighty and the Powerful.

'Abdu'l-Bahá

PRAYERS OF WOMEN

*Undoubtedly the greatest glory of women is servitude
at His threshold and submissiveness at His door; it is
the possession of a vigilant heart, and praise of the
incomparable God . . .*

'Abdu'l-Bahá

O GOD, my God! This Thy handmaid is calling upon Thee, trusting in Thee, turning her face unto Thee, imploring Thee to shed Thy heavenly bounties upon her, and to disclose unto her Thy spiritual mysteries, and to cast upon her the lights of Thy Godhead.

O my Lord! Make the eyes of my husband to see. Rejoice his heart with the light of the knowledge of Thee, draw Thou his mind unto Thy luminous beauty, cheer Thou his spirit by revealing unto him Thy manifest splendours.

O my Lord! Lift Thou the veil from before his sight. Rain down Thy plenteous bounties upon him, intoxicate him with the wine of love for Thee, make him one of Thy angels whose feet walk upon this earth even as their souls are soaring through the high heavens. Cause him to become a brilliant lamp, shining out with the light of Thy wisdom in the midst of Thy people.

Verily, Thou art the Precious, the Ever-Bestowing, the Open of Hand.

'Abdu'l-Bahá

MY LORD! My Lord! I praise Thee and I thank Thee for that whereby Thou hast favoured Thine humble maidservant, Thy slave beseeching and supplicating Thee, because Thou hast verily guided her unto Thine obvious Kingdom and caused her to hear Thine exalted Call in the contingent world and to behold Thy signs which prove the appearance of Thy victorious reign over all things.

O my Lord, I dedicate that which is in my womb unto Thee. Then cause it to be a praiseworthy child in Thy Kingdom and a fortunate one by Thy favour and Thy generosity; to develop and to grow up under the charge of Thine education. Verily, Thou art the Gracious! Verily, Thou art the Lord of Great Favour!

'Abdu'l-Bahá

PRAYERS FOR MARRIAGE

In this glorious Cause the life of a married couple should resemble the life of the angels in heaven — a life full of joy and spiritual delight, a life of unity and concord . . .

'Abdu'l-Bahá

HE IS the Bestower, the Bounteous!

Praise be to God, the Ancient, the Ever-Abiding, the Changeless, the Eternal! He Who hath testified in His Own Being that verily he is the One, the Single, the Untrammelled, the Exalted. We bear witness that verily there is no God but Him, acknowledging His oneness, confessing His singleness. He hath ever dwelt in unapproachable heights, in the summits of His loftiness, sanctified from the mention of aught save Himself, free from the description of aught but Him.

And when He desired to manifest grace and beneficence to men, and to set the world in order, He revealed observances and created laws; among them He established the law of marriage, made it as a fortress for well-being and salvation, and enjoined it upon us in that which was sent down out of the heaven of sanctity in His Most Holy Book. He saith, great is His glory: 'Marry, O people, that from you may appear he who will remember Me amongst My servants; this is one of My commandments unto you; obey it as an assistance to yourselves.'

Bahá'u'lláh

HE IS GOD!

O peerless Lord! In Thine almighty wisdom Thou hast enjoined marriage upon the peoples, that the generations of men may succeed one another in this contingent world, and that ever, so long as the world shall last, they may busy themselves at the Threshold of Thy oneness with servitude and worship, with salutation, adoration and praise. 'I have not created spirits and men but that they should worship me.' Wherefore, wed Thou in the heaven of Thy mercy these two birds of the nest of Thy love, and make them the means of attracting perpetual grace; that from the union of these two seas of love a wave of tenderness may surge and cast the pearls of pure and goodly issue on the shore of life. 'He hath let loose the two seas, that they meet each other: Between them is a barrier which they overpass not. Which then of the bounties of your Lord will ye deny? From each He bringeth up greater and lesser pearls.'

O Thou kind Lord! Make Thou this marriage to bring forth coral and pearls. Thou art verily the All-Powerful, the Most Great, the Ever-Forgiving.

'Abdu'l-Bahá

O MY LORD, O my Lord! These two bright moons are wedded in Thy love, conjoined in servitude to Thy Holy Threshold, united in ministering to Thy Cause. Make Thou this marriage to be as threading lights of Thine abounding grace, O my Lord, the All-Merciful, and luminous rays of Thy bestowals, O Thou the Beneficent, the Ever-Giving, that there may branch out from this great tree boughs that will grow green and flourishing through the gifts that rain down from Thy clouds of grace.

Verily, Thou art the Generous. Verily, Thou art the Almighty. Verily, Thou art the Compassionate, the All-Merciful.   *'Abdu'l-Bahá*

GLORY be unto Thee, O my God! Verily, this Thy servant and this Thy maidservant have gathered under the shadow of Thy mercy and they are united through Thy favour and generosity. O Lord! Assist them in this Thy world and Thy kingdom and destine for them every good through Thy bounty and grace. O Lord! Confirm them in Thy servitude and assist them in Thy service. Suffer them to become the signs of Thy Name in Thy world and protect them through Thy bestowals which are inexhaustible in this world and the world to come. O Lord! They are supplicating the kingdom of Thy mercifulness and invoking the realm of Thy singleness. Verily, they are married in obedience to Thy command. Cause them to become the signs of harmony and unity until the end of time. Verily, Thou art the Omnipotent, the Omnipresent and the Almighty.   *'Abdu'l-Bahá*